CAMPING JOURNAL FOR KIDS

CAMPING JOURNAL
➤➤ FOR KIDS ⬅⬅

RECORD YOUR ADVENTURES
IN THE GREAT OUTDOORS

KIM ANDREWS

ILLUSTRATIONS BY CAIT BRENNAN

ROCKRIDGE
PRESS

For general information on our other products and services or to obtain technical support, please contact our Customer Care Department within the United States at (866) 744-2665, or outside the United States at (510) 253-0500.

Rockridge Press publishes its books in a variety of electronic and print formats. Some content that appears in print may not be available in electronic books, and vice versa.

TRADEMARKS: Rockridge Press and the Rockridge Press logo are trademarks or registered trademarks of Callisto Media Inc. and/or its affiliates, in the United States and other countries, and may not be used without written permission. All other trademarks are the property of their respective owners. Rockridge Press is not associated with any product or vendor mentioned in this book.

Interior and Cover Designer: Sean Doyle
Art Producer: Sue Bischofberger
Editor: Eliza Kirby
Production Editor: Sigi Nacson
Production Manager: Martin Worthington

Illustrations: © 2021 Cait Brennan

ISBN: 978-1-63807-325-3
R0

Here's to Being a Happy Camper!

Camping is a fun and adventurous way to experience the earth's natural wonders. This camping journal helps you keep track of all your outstanding nature trips! In the first section of this book are facts and information that may come in handy as you hike and explore. The rest of the book is for journaling—about your camping spots, any wacky (or normal) weather, the critters you encounter, and other wonderful things you see or do along the way. Just toss this journal into your backpack, and go make some memories!

THE CAMPER'S TOOL KIT

These "tools" start you on the trail to being a junior naturalist in no time! Learn to look at the world in weird and wild new ways, discover creative camping tips and techniques, and embark on invigorating adventures.

Read the Sky

Observing the clouds, sun, stars, and moon can give you helpful clues when hiking, playing, exploring, and camping outdoors. For campers who know what to look for, the sky shows weather patterns, tells you the time, and even holds navigational secrets!

BY DAY

Learning to identify common cloud types gives you a general idea of the weather to expect. That way you can better map out your activities. Wispy cirrus clouds or fluffy cumulus clouds likely mean sunny skies—a great day for a hike! Flat, layered stratus clouds or dark, low-lying nimbus clouds say rain is possibly in the forecast, so you may want to cover your camp area with a tarp for extra protection.

BY NIGHT

On a clear night, countless stars twinkle in the night sky. If you play connect-the-dots with the stars, you might imagine different images. Some clusters of stars that form images, such as the Crab and the Harp, are called "constellations." Because the earth is always rotating, where you live and the current season determine what star clusters you see.

One star, however, always appears in the same spot. This star is Polaris, nicknamed "the North Star." It's visible year-round in the Northern Hemisphere sky. Polaris always marks the direction north. To find Polaris, first locate the Big Dipper. The two stars at the far end of the Big Dipper's bowl point to Polaris—it's the bright star at the tip of the Little Dipper's handle.

You might also want to chart the moon cycle in your journal. Just like the sun, the moon provides a directional compass—both always rise in the east and set in the west. When the moon is full, which happens roughly once a month, it provides the perfect lighting for a night walk with your group.

SETTING SUN

If you are out on an adventure, make sure you get back to camp before nightfall! If you know it will be dark soon, use your hands to estimate how long until the sun sets.

Extend your arm out toward the sun, positioning your hand so it's parallel with the horizon. Count the number of fingers between the sun and the horizon. Each finger represents about fifteen minutes until the sun goes down.

Take a Nature Walk

The best way to gather information about new places is to explore! Take a nature walk to discover the plants and wildlife in each new area you camp. Gather a few supplies in your backpack, like a water bottle, snacks, a first-aid kit, this camping journal and a pencil, a whistle (to signal for help in case of an emergency), a rain poncho, and a flashlight. You might also want to carry a field guide for identifying nature.

When on your nature walk, notice the surroundings. What do you see, hear, and smell? Use your journal to sketch pictures and write descriptions of the plants, animals, and scenery. Do you see anything curious or unidentifiable? Write these down in your journal to research later. Stay away from anything dangerous, like large animals, snakes, poisonous plants, and rushing water!

TREES AND LEAVES

Take a look around your campsite. Are there any trees? If so, pick at least one to observe closely. What does the bark on its trunk look and feel like? Do you notice any insects crawling on the tree? How about the color and shape of the leaves? Look for any tree seeds on the ground, such as acorns, pine cones, or prickly pods, called sweet gum balls.

Journaling these details helps you identify the many different trees you see when camping. There are two types of trees—deciduous and evergreen. Deciduous trees, like an oak or red maple, have leaves that change color in autumn before falling to the ground. Evergreen trees, such as fir and pine trees, have needles that stay green all year long.

Maple

Sycamore

Beech

Elder

Oak

Birch

Horse Chestnut

PLANTS AND FLOWERS

Height, color, scent, leaves, and petals are all helpful hints for identifying flowers and plants. You may be surprised to discover so many interesting—and strange—varieties. You might see a Venus flytrap (yes, it actually eats flies!) on the Carolina coast, or an edible prickly pear cactus in the desert. Each area you explore has plants that are unique to that place. Plants of a particular region or habitat are called "flora." If you come across a lot of a certain plant or flower, it's usually fine to pick one to press into your journal. If there are only a few, however, please leave them be. Find out if there are restrictions for plucking flora in the area, especially on protected nature preserves. A park ranger or field guide can help you learn the names of the flowers you find.

LEAVES OF THREE

Have you ever heard the saying "Leaves of three, let them be"? This clever rhyme is a reminder to stay away from poison oak and poison ivy. Both plants have leaves that stem off in sets of three. Both also cause blisters and itching to the skin in about 85 percent of people. An itchy rash could cramp your camping fun!

Poison ivy's jagged leaves have pointy tips, and it is often found as a vine climbing up trees. But it can also cover the ground or grow as an individual plant. Poison oak usually grows as a shrub, and its leaves have rounded, lobed edges. Both plants may turn from green to yellow, orange, or red in the fall.

If you think you've had a brush with poison oak or ivy, use a washcloth and dish soap to clean the areas it touched. Also, the plants' oils can be transferred to pets, so if your dog rubs against poison ivy, give him a good scrubbing. Those oils can spread to you, too, so wear rubber gloves!

Observe Wildlife

Spotting wild animals can be exciting on a camping trip! Birds and squirrels are usually easy to spot, but many critters prefer to hide and sneak out only occasionally. Early morning, when the world outdoors is still quiet, is a great time to peek outside your tent. Sit quietly, and look for any animals coming out to find breakfast. Just be sure it isn't *your* breakfast—always keep food packed away. A raccoon is fun to watch in the woods, but not if he's tearing open the loaf of bread you were going to turn into campfire French toast!

Wild animals are protective of their babies, food, and homes, so do not disturb—observe only from a distance. Stay 25 feet away from small animals and 100 feet from larger animals. Bears are not as snuggly as they look.

ANIMAL TRACKS

Identifying animal tracks, or footprints, is great for discovering local wildlife. If you come across animal tracks, notice how deep they are in the ground. The heavier the animal is, the deeper its tracks. Also note the overall shape, pattern of steps, and number of toes.

Raccoon tracks somewhat resemble baby hands. Raccoon hands are two to three inches wide and have five fingers, the hind paw being a tad larger than the front paw. Their handlike paws

help them open jars, untie knots, and lift trash can lids, which is why raccoons like to frequent campsites!

Another common animal track to spot is from a deer. Deer may even use the same paths you do when walking through the woods! Their cloven hooves create tracks that resemble upside-down hearts.

SCAT IDENTIFICATION

"Scat" is a word for animal droppings or poop, and identifying it is another way to learn what animals live nearby. When journaling scat details, take note of the following: size, shape, smell, wetness or dryness, and what's in it (look—don't touch!).

Rabbit scat, as an example, is round and very small—less than one centimeter. It usually looks dry, and may have bits of plant

or grass pieces. Deer poop is similar, but smoother and more oval-shaped. If you spot scat about two inches long with pointy ends on rocks, stumps, or logs, it likely belongs to a fox. It may have bits of hair, bone, seeds, or berries mixed in.

NATURE STROLL BINGO

How many of these things can you spot on a stroll around your campsite? Play a bingo-type game by checking off each box as you find items. Can you get four in a row?

SOMETHING SMOOTH	MUSHROOM	ACORN	PINE CONE
FLAT ROCK	SOMETHING FUZZY	Y-SHAPED STICK	INSECT
RED LEAF	SOMETHING BUMPY	SPIDERWEB	SONGBIRD
MOSS	WORM	ANIMAL SCAT	SOMETHING WET

LEAVE NO TRACE

"Leave no trace" is a saying that helps you remember to enjoy nature without disturbing it. Use the principles below when you're camping.

Plan and prep ahead. Bring plenty of food and water, prepare for expected weather conditions, find out if campfires are allowed, and arrive during daylight to safely set up camp.

Properly dispose of waste. Trash, fishing lines, and even your poop can be harmful to wildlife. Place all garbage in a trash can with a secure lid. If you do not have access to a public bathroom, dig a hole for poop and bury it!

Do not disturb. If possible, try not to break sticks, disturb piles of leaves, or move rocks around. These are important nature items for many creatures.

Minimize campfire impact. Do not build a fire during high winds or extremely dry weather, and always use water to douse your fire completely before leaving.

Help keep nature clean. When hiking, bring along a grocery bag in your pocket or backpack to collect trash from the trails.

Respect wildlife. Do not feed, touch, or go near wild animals. You could harm them and their habitats—and they could harm you.

Leave what you find. Try to leave the campsite exactly as you found it when you arrived.

How to Use This Journal

These journal pages offer a fun way to record special memories from your camping trips. Keep track of the dates and locations of your adventures, weather patterns, and your camping companions. There's also room for notes and sketches, to write and draw about your experiences—anything goes! You'll find helpful tips scattered throughout the pages. A sample journal entry is provided here, and what follows is a breakdown of its sections to guide you. Happy camp journaling!

DATE: April 12, 2021

LOCATION: Hanging Rock State Park (Site #40), North Carolina

WEATHER: It was sunny and warm (about 75 degrees F), but sometimes it felt colder because it was so windy—especially at the top of the mountain!

CAMPING WITH: My aunt, uncle, and cousin

FIELD NOTES: We hiked all the way to the top of Hanging Rock. It was so high! Later I ate a giant s'more and got chocolate all over my face. My cousin and I slept in hammock tents and could hear animals at night. It was a little creepy but so cool!

Camping Tip

Bring glow stick necklaces! Wear them while playing outside after dark, place them by tent stakes so you don't trip, or hang them in your tent as night-lights.

DATE

In this section you can record the date of your camping trip. You may even want to note what season it is. By writing down these details you can discover what time of year you enjoy camping the most!

LOCATION

Write down where you are camping. Include the name of the campground, park, mountain, or lake; your campsite number; what city or state you are in; and any other information about the location, like how many miles it is from your home.

WEATHER

Here you will make notes about the weather. Write down the temperature and if it was sunny, cloudy, rainy, or snowy. Perhaps it was a sunny 70 degrees, but then you climbed to the top of a mountain, and it was 40 degrees, foggy, and windy—you might want to bring a warmer coat next time! Write all of those details here.

CAMPING WITH

Name the people you are camping with and anything you want to remember about them. For example:

- *Uncle Doug snored really loud—next time I'll bring earplugs!*

- *Caleb, Savannah, and Connor shared my tent, and we played cards. I won!*

- *Nana made the best crab soup. I want her to teach me the recipe.*

FIELD NOTES

Write about your camping experience—favorite memories, yummiest foods, and the exciting things you saw and did—in the field notes section. Here are some ideas to get you started:

- Record your favorite and least favorite part of the day or trip.

- Write about someone new you met while camping.

- Jot down a note about something you wished you had packed, but didn't.

- Describe your favorite campfire meal.

- Write about something that made you laugh.

- Make a list of any animals or critters you saw or heard on your trip.

- What sounds did you hear while you were falling asleep?

- Tell about something you discovered while exploring.

SKETCH

This space is for sketching what you see and do on your trip. You can also get creative with stamps and stickers, or tape things here like a trip photo, postcard, camp brochure, four-leaf clover, or even a colorful leaf you find. Your journal will be special and unique—just like you!

Try these fun ideas:

- Pick a color. Look around and draw what you see of that color.

- Tape the most colorful leaf you can find onto a page.

- Fill a page with drawings of any animal footprints that you see.

- Sketch a map of the area, including mountains, bodies of water, trails, and camping areas.

- Create a space with drawings of birds you spot on your trip.

- Draw the night sky and any constellations you see. What did the moon look like?

- Draw and describe a thunderstorm. What did you see, hear, and smell?

- Lie on the ground and observe the clouds. Do any of the clouds look like animals or objects? Draw them in your journal!

- Draw a picture of your campfire: What colors do you see? Try adding a copper pipe with a piece of garden hose inside to your fire. Now what colors appear?

- Take a leaf and place it vein-side up behind one of your journal pages. Holding a crayon on its side (with the paper removed), rub back and forth watching the leaf take shape on your paper.

CAMPING TIPS

Throughout the book, at the bottom of some of your journal pages, you'll find tips and tricks for savvy campers.

SAFETY FIRST

Whether you are camping at the beach, on top of a mountain, in a hammock in the woods, or at a national park campsite, the most important factor is *safety*! Be a cautious camper by following these safety tips:

Carry a backpack with safety and exploring essentials.

Always have an adult nearby when playing in water or near fire.

Move slowly away from any wild animals you encounter.

Poison mushrooms, berries, and plants are to be avoided.

Insect repellent should be worn to prevent tick and mosquito bites.

Never explore alone, and let an adult know where you are going.

Get out of the way of bikers, horses, or wild animals when you're hiking.

YOUR CAMPING JOURNAL

In this section are journal pages for your camping adventures. Each page includes suggestions for what to record, but there is also plenty of space for notes, sketches, and other creativity!

○ DATE: --

🌳 LOCATION: --

🌤 WEATHER: --

🎒 CAMPING WITH: ----------------------------------

✎ FIELD NOTES: ------------------------------------

Camping Tip

Play tic-tac-toe wherever you go! Find four sticks of similar size to form a grid. You and your partner each need five game tokens. You can use rocks, and your friend can use acorns; or, one can use white shells, and the other can use all black—whatever you find!

SKETCH:

○ DATE:
_____

🌳 LOCATION:
_____

_____

⛅ WEATHER:
_____

_____

🎒 CAMPING WITH:
_____

_____

📝 FIELD NOTES:
_____

_____

_____

_____

_____

_____

_____

_____

_____

_____

SKETCH:

DATE: _____

 LOCATION: _____
 _____

 WEATHER: _____
 _____
 _____

 CAMPING WITH: _____
 _____
 _____

 FIELD NOTES: _____
 _____
 _____
 _____
 _____

Camping Tip

Have you ever heard the silly idea that garlic scares off
vampires? Although vampires aren't real, it turns out that
garlic can be helpful in repelling something else—mosquitoes!
You can crush bits of garlic in mineral oil and rub it on
your skin. The smell might scare away the bugs—or maybe
even humans.

SKETCH:

DATE: _____

LOCATION: _____

WEATHER: _____

_____

CAMPING WITH: _____

_____

FIELD NOTES: _____

_____

_____

_____

_____

_____

_____

_____

SKETCH:

O DATE:

🌳 LOCATION:

🌄 WEATHER:

🎒 CAMPING WITH:

✏️ FIELD NOTES:

Camping Tip

Hike in areas that are safe and have solid ground, where
you won't disturb wildlife, and stick to trails when possible.
A walking stick helps you balance along rocky or uneven ter-
rain. A stick is also great for clearing spiderwebs off the path,
and checking for critters in long grass and under leaf piles.

SKETCH:

DATE:

LOCATION:

WEATHER:

CAMPING WITH:

FIELD NOTES:

SKETCH:

O DATE: _____

LOCATION: _____
_____

WEATHER: _____
_____
_____

CAMPING WITH: _____
_____
_____

FIELD NOTES: _____
_____
_____
_____
_____

Camping Tip

Go on an alphabet scavenger hunt. Explore the campsite, looking for items that begin with each letter of the alphabet: A is for acorn, ant, or apple; B is for backpack, bee, or bird; C is for camper or creek; D is for dandelion or dirt; and so on.

SKETCH:

DATE: _____

LOCATION: _____
_____

WEATHER: _____
_____
_____

CAMPING WITH: _____
_____
_____

FIELD NOTES: _____
_____
_____
_____
_____
_____
_____
_____
_____
_____
_____

○ DATE: _____

🌳 LOCATION: _____
_____

☁ WEATHER: _____
_____
_____

🎒 CAMPING WITH: _____
_____
_____

✏ FIELD NOTES: _____
_____
_____
_____
_____
_____

Camping Tip

Catching fireflies makes summer nights magical. For a makeshift lantern, gently put them in jars with bits of grass and a damp piece of paper towel. No need to poke holes in the lid—there's plenty of air for them to breathe until you set them free at bedtime.

SKETCH:

○ DATE: --

🌳 LOCATION: ------------------------------------

☁ WEATHER: -------------------------------------

🎒 CAMPING WITH: --------------------------------

✏ FIELD NOTES: ---------------------------------

SKETCH:

DATE:

LOCATION:

WEATHER:

CAMPING WITH:

FIELD NOTES:

Camping Tip

Never keep snacks inside your tent. Store food in sealed
containers to deter unwanted critters such as ants, flies,
bees, raccoons, or even bears . . . oh my!

SKETCH:

DATE: _____

LOCATION: _____
_____

WEATHER: _____
_____

CAMPING WITH: _____
_____

FIELD NOTES: _____
_____
_____
_____
_____
_____
_____
_____
_____
_____

SKETCH:

○ DATE: _____

🌳 LOCATION: _____
_____

⛰ WEATHER: _____
_____
_____

🎒 CAMPING WITH: _____
_____
_____

✏ FIELD NOTES: _____
_____
_____
_____
_____
_____

Camping Tip

Bring binoculars. A good pair of binoculars helps you get a
closer and clearer look at the scenery, wildlife, and stars.
Do *not* look directly at the sun; it can hurt your vision.

SKETCH:

O DATE: _____

🌳 LOCATION: _____
_____

🌄 WEATHER: _____
_____
_____

🎒 CAMPING WITH: _____
_____
_____

✏️ FIELD NOTES: _____
_____
_____
_____
_____
_____
_____
_____
_____
_____

SKETCH:

○ DATE:

♣ LOCATION:

● WEATHER:

● CAMPING WITH:

✎ FIELD NOTES:

Camping Tip

Look for a smooth bark tree with moss growing up its trunk.
You've likely determined which way is north. The north side
of the tree gets less sunlight and has more moisture—moss
loves that!

SKETCH:

DATE: _____

LOCATION: _____
_____

WEATHER: _____
_____

CAMPING WITH: _____
_____

FIELD NOTES: _____
_____
_____
_____
_____
_____
_____
_____
_____
_____

DATE: --

LOCATION: ------------------------------------

WEATHER: ------------------------------------

CAMPING WITH: ------------------------------

FIELD NOTES: --------------------------------

SKETCH:

O DATE: _____

🌳 LOCATION: _____

_____

☁️ WEATHER: _____

_____

_____

🎒 CAMPING WITH: _____

_____

_____

📝 FIELD NOTES: _____

_____

_____

_____

_____

_____

Camping Tip

It's always good to have some trail mix on hand. Toss a combo of snacks—like nuts, chocolate, dried fruit, sunflower seeds, and beef jerky—into a sandwich bag and shake it up. Just remember not to leave food behind—dropping trail mix might lead to a trail of animals behind you!

SKETCH:

O DATE: _____

🌳 LOCATION: _____
_____

☁ WEATHER: _____
_____
_____

🎒 CAMPING WITH: _____
_____
_____

✒ FIELD NOTES: _____
_____
_____
_____
_____
_____
_____
_____
_____
_____
_____

SKETCH:

○ DATE:

🌳 LOCATION:

🌅 WEATHER:

🎒 CAMPING WITH:

✏️ FIELD NOTES:

Camping Tip

When you wake up in the morning, do you see tiny water droplets on the blades of grass? This is dew, and it usually means the day ahead will be clear and sunny.

SKETCH:

DATE: ....

LOCATION: ....

....

WEATHER: ....

....

....

CAMPING WITH: ....

....

....

FIELD NOTES: ....

....

....

....

....

....

....

....

....

....

....

SKETCH:

DATE:
_____

LOCATION:
_____

WEATHER:
_____

_____

CAMPING WITH:
_____

_____

FIELD NOTES:
_____

_____

_____

_____

_____

_____

_____

_____

_____

⏱ DATE: ....

🌳 LOCATION: ....

....

⛅ WEATHER: ....

....

....

🎒 CAMPING WITH: ....

....

....

✏️ FIELD NOTES: ....

....

....

....

....

....

Camping Tip

Try geocaching. Using GPS coordinates, you can navigate to different locations to find "treasures." Read more online or download the geocaching app on your phone.

SKETCH:

O DATE: --

LOCATION: ---

WEATHER: --

CAMPING WITH: ---------------------------------

FIELD NOTES: --------------------------------------

SKETCH:

○ DATE: _____

🌳 LOCATION: _____

☁ WEATHER: _____
_____
_____

🎒 CAMPING WITH: _____
_____
_____

✏ FIELD NOTES: _____
_____
_____
_____
_____
_____

Camping Tip

Do you hear froggy tunes? A rainstorm is likely looming.
Frogs typically stay in water to keep moist, but before a
storm, they often come out to enjoy the extra moisture
in the air.

SKETCH:

DATE:

LOCATION:

WEATHER:

CAMPING WITH:

FIELD NOTES:

SKETCH:

DATE: _____

LOCATION: _____
_____

WEATHER: _____
_____
_____

CAMPING WITH: _____
_____
_____

FIELD NOTES: _____
_____
_____
_____
_____
_____
_____
_____
_____
_____
_____

SKETCH:

○ DATE: _____

🌳 LOCATION: _____

☁ WEATHER: _____

_____

_____

🎒 CAMPING WITH: _____

_____

_____

✏ FIELD NOTES: _____

_____

_____

_____

_____

_____

Camping Tip

Right before the sun sets, incredible color ribbons happen
in the sky: pinks, oranges, reds, and purples. Also observe
how the treetops are shady on the bottom and sunny
on top.

SKETCH:

DATE:

LOCATION:

WEATHER:

CAMPING WITH:

FIELD NOTES:

SKETCH:

O DATE:

LOCATION:

WEATHER:

CAMPING WITH:

FIELD NOTES:

Camping Tip

Roasting hot dogs on a stick? Put out a toppings bar! Set the picnic table with the usual rolls and condiments, but also chili beans, shredded cheese, bacon bits, chopped peppers and onion, pickled relish, slaw or kraut, and sliced avocado. Use leftovers later—loaded onto baked potatoes!

SKETCH:

O DATE: _____

🌳 LOCATION: _____

_____

⛅ WEATHER: _____

_____

_____

🎒 CAMPING WITH: _____

_____

_____

✏️ FIELD NOTES: _____

_____

_____

_____

_____

_____

_____

_____

_____

_____

_____

SKETCH:

DATE: -

LOCATION: -

- -

WEATHER: -

- -

- -

CAMPING WITH: -

- -

- -

FIELD NOTES: -

- -

- -

- -

- -

- -

- -

- -

○ DATE: _____

🌳 LOCATION: _____

_____

🌤 WEATHER: _____

_____

_____

🎒 CAMPING WITH: _____

_____

_____

📝 FIELD NOTES: _____

_____

_____

_____

_____

_____

Camping Tip

Embrace rainy weather with mud play! Splash in puddles, paint your face and arms with designs, serve pretend "coffee" and mud pies to your family.

SKETCH:

○ DATE: ---

🌳 LOCATION: ---

🌥 WEATHER: --

🎒 CAMPING WITH: ---------------------------------------

✏️ FIELD NOTES: ---------------------------------------

SKETCH:

MY NOTES

These additional lined pages are perfect for writing out your trip plans, places you want to go, strange or interesting dreams you have, or a favorite memory. You can also make lists, such as names of new friends, birds you see, mountains you hike, or wild animals you spot!

About the Author

 **Kim Andrews** is a North Carolina–based author, teacher, and blogger. She is devoted to nature-based education, and writes about her passion for exploring, crafting, and outdoor learning at LearningBarefoot.com.